# WORLD WAR II

A Cherrytree Book

Designed and produced by
A S Publishing

First published 1988
by Cherrytree Press Ltd
327 High St
Slough
Berkshire SL1 1TX

Reprinted 1989, 1994, 1997
First Softcover edition
Reprinted 1997, 1999, 2001

Copyright this edition © Evans Brothers Ltd 2001

*British Library Cataloguing in Publication Data*
Hills, Ken
  World War II.—(Wars that changed the
  world).
  1. World War, 1939-1945
  I. Title II. Berry, John
  III. Series
  940.53        D743

  ISBN 0-7451-5007-1 (Hardcover)
  ISBN 1-84234-085-9 (Softcover)

Printed in Italy by New Interlitho, Milano

# WARS THAT CHANGED THE WORLD

# WORLD WAR II

*By* Ken Hills
*Illustrated by* John Berry

CHERRYTREE BOOKS

# The Coming of War

At dawn on 1 September 1939, German armies marched into Poland. On 3 September, Britain and France were at war with their old enemy, Germany.

Adolf Hitler, head of the Nazi party, had come to power in 1933. He had killed or imprisoned his enemies and set out to make Germany the leading nation in Europe. Secretly he had built up his armed forces. In 1938, he took part of Czechoslovakia and seized the whole of Austria. Britain and France protested, but when Hitler promised not to invade any more territory, they agreed he could keep what he had already taken.

Promises meant nothing to Hitler. Next year he sent his armies into Poland which Britain and France had promised to help if she were invaded. This time they stood firm. When Hitler refused to withdraw, they declared war on Germany.

## The Opening Moves

Before he attacked Poland, Hitler had done a deal with the Russian leader, Joseph Stalin. Rather than fight each other over Poland, they would share it between them. Five German armies invaded Poland. It took them only eighteen days to conquer the country.

In the West, the French and British allies faced the German armies. Nothing happened for six months. This period was called *sitzkrieg*, or the phoney war.

The action came in the North. On 9 April 1940, without warning, the Germans invaded Denmark and Norway. French and British troops, sent hastily by sea to drive them out, were easily beaten off. Germany now controlled a vast coastline from which to threaten Britain.

Adolf Hitler was the leader of Germany. He kept himself in power by murdering or terrorising everyone who opposed him. His greatest crime was his attempt to kill the whole Jewish people.

Hitler's main ally was another dictator, Benito Mussolini, the leader of Italy.

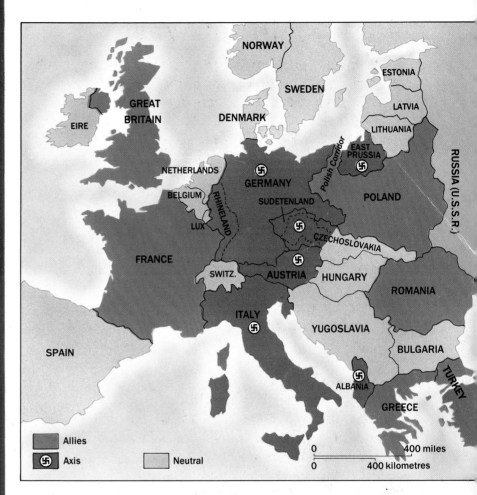

| | |
|---|---|
| Allies | |
| Axis | Neutral |

0        400 miles
0        400 kilometres

The swastika is an ancient form of cross. The name means 'good luck'. Hitler took it as the badge of the Nazi party. When he came to power, the swastika became the national sign of Germany. Germany and her allies were kown as the Axis powers.

The map shows Europe at the outbreak of the war. When no-one tried to stop him, Hitler believed it was safe to grab more territory. He attacked Poland in 1939 to join the two parts of Germany together, which had been separated since World War I.

# Blitzkrieg

When the Second World War began, most people assumed that it would be fought like the First. The war would be won by the side with the strongest fortifications and the greatest firepower. It would be a war of defence, not attack.

The Germans believed differently. They worked out a new way of fighting, using fast-moving armoured vehicles. They called it *blitzkrieg*, or lightning war.

Blitzkrieg employed masses of tanks, supported by artillery, to punch holes in enemy defences. Troops in armoured carriers poured through these gaps and drove deep into enemy territory. The enemy troops in the front line were thus cut off from their supplies and easily defeated.

It was essential to command the air over the battlefield. Aircraft were used to support the advancing tanks once they had passed beyond the range of their own artillery.

General Guderian was the foremost German expert in this new warfare. He led the Panzer (armoured) divisions which caused the fall of France in 1940.

Stukas played a vital role in blitzkrieg warfare. They were used as flying artillery to support the Panzers on the ground. They dived almost vertically on their targets and could bomb with tremendous accuracy.

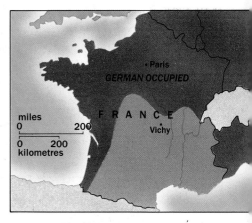

The Germans allowed part of France to be ruled from Vichy by the aged First World War hero Marshal Pétain. The Free French fought on from Britain, under General de Gaulle.

The victorious German army marches through Paris (right), under the Arc de Triomphe, in June 1940.

## The Fall of France

Without warning, the Germans invaded Holland and Belgium. The German airforce, the Luftwaffe, prepared the way for the army with bombing raids and by dropping paratroops to capture key roads and bridges. The Dutch and Belgians fought bravely, but had no answer to the speed and surprise of blitzkrieg warfare. In four days, the German Panzers had burst through their defences and swept on to France to meet the French and British.

A German army group cut the Allied line and turned towards the Channel, trapping the British force on the coast near Dunkirk. The rest raced on, brushing aside resistance, until they reached the Atlantic shores of France. The French were forced to ask for peace.

The Germans occupied the whole length of the northern and western coastline of France. They used it as a base from which to attack Britain and British shipping.

### DUNKIRK

Nine days of continuous flat calm is a rare event in the English Channel. But it happened when a host of little pleasure boats went with the Royal Navy to the Dunkirk beaches, to bring home British troops trapped there. The planners reckoned that, if the RAF could keep the Luftwaffe at bay, 35,000 men might be saved in two days. In the end, over 330,000 British and Allied soldiers were rescued. No wonder it was called at the time 'The Miracle of Dunkirk'.

# The Battle of Britain

At times of greatest danger and crisis, the British people gathered round their radio sets to hear the defiant words of Prime Minister Winston Churchill (1874-1965). He was a strong leader, utterly dedicated to Britain, and to the defeat of Hitler's Germany.

By mid-October, the RAF was still unconquered, and autumn gales were blowing in the Channel. Hitler called off the invasion.

Churchill taunted him over the radio 'We are waiting for the long planned invasion,' he said. 'So are the fishes.'

France was out of the war by June 1940 and Hitler's next target was Britain. He planned an invasion under the code name Operation Sealion, to be completed before winter set in. Fleets of troop-carrying barges were massed along the French coast and Hitler ordered, 'Win control of the Channel. Destroy the Royal Air Force.' In Churchill's words, 'The Battle of Britain was about to begin.'

The Luftwaffe began by bombing ships in the Channel, but soon switched the attack to the RAF itself. On 13 August, which Hitler named Eagle Day, the Luftwaffe raided fighter bases in southern England. Much damage was done, but German plans were already going wrong.

The British Spitfire was proving a better fighter than the German Messerschmitt 109. As the battle went on, German losses grew and there was no sign whatever of the British giving in. Luftwaffe pilots were told that the RAF was down to its last few fighters, but when they crossed the British coast, swarms rose to meet them. The morale of the German airmen began to fall.

## The London Blitz

Then Hitler decided to attack London. This was terrible for Londoners, but it gave the RAF time to repair the damage done to its airfields. On 15 September, the Germans threw nearly 1000 aircraft into a final desperate attempt to overcome the RAF. The Luftwaffe lost 60 aircraft; the RAF lost 26. The Germans had failed.

Hitler was now convinced he could not invade Britain and called off Operation Sealion. He had lost his first battle. A few hundred young fighter pilots had saved Britain. It was a turning point in the war.

**Spitfire Mark II**
Fighter
Speed 357 mph (574 km/h)
8 machine-guns

**Hurricane Mark I**
Fighter
Speed 328 mph (528 km/h)
8 machine-guns

**Messerschmitt 109E**
Fighter
Speed 354 mph (570 km/h)
2 cannon
2 machine-guns

**Heinkel III**
Bomber
Speed 258 mph (415 km/h)
Bomb load 5510 lbs (2500 kg)

# The Invasion of Russia

In the winter of 1940, after he had failed to conquer Britain, Hitler ordered his generals to plan the invasion of Russia. If he could overcome Russia, all Europe would lie under German control and he could then turn all his power against his remaining enemies, the British. Over 3 million German troops were massed on the Russian border, and on 22 June 1941 they invaded Russia.

At first everything went to plan. The Russians were in retreat everywhere. Hundreds of thousands were killed or captured. Half the Russian airforce had been destroyed.

By 30 September, 14 Panzer divisions were poised to move against the Russian capital Moscow. But then the weather changed. The Panzers bogged down completely in mud caused by heavy rain. Worse was to come: the Russian winter.

Marshal Georgi Zhukov (1896-1974) was the mastermind behind the Russian defeat of the German armies. He was known as 'The General who never lost a battle'.

## OPERATION BARBAROSSA

Hitler code-named the attack on Russia 'Operation Barbarossa'. The German armies attacked Russia on three fronts. In the north, the target was Leningrad. In the centre, it was the capital Moscow. In the south, the Germans set out to capture Russian oilfields and corn-growing lands.

Using blitzkrieg tactics, the Luftwaffe destroyed 1800 Russian aircraft in the first few days of battle – most of them still on the ground.

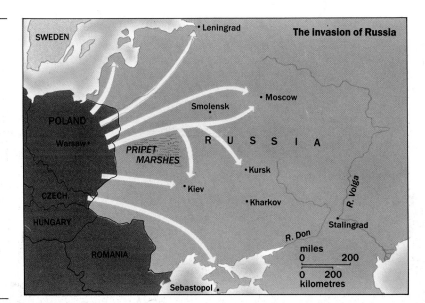

The invasion of Russia

## The Russian Winter

In the terrible Russian winter, temperatures do not rise above minus 21°C for many weeks. The Germans were totally unprepared for such conditions. Tank engines froze solid. Gunsights were made useless. Men in summer clothing froze to death.

The Russian forces were used to fighting in winter. They were also growing stronger. New factories had been set up in Russia's Asian territories, far away and safe from German attack. They began to pour out quantities of new up-to-date weapons. Millions of fresh soldiers from these Asian lands were joining the fight.

On 6 December, Marshal Zhukov, commanding the Russian armies, launched a great counter-attack. Moscow was saved and the Germans retreated everywhere. They were not beaten yet, but blitzkrieg warfare had suffered its first major defeat.

The T34 tank was Russia's answer to the German Panzers. It was the best tank of its time and no German gun could pierce its thick, sloping armour. Here a T34 is literally crushing some German opposition.

# The Rise of Japan

Japan wanted to become the leading power in Asia so she set out to win an empire. In 1931 she occupied Korea and Manchuria. She made war on China and seized large areas of her territory. When France was defeated in 1940, Japan took her colonies in South East Asia.

The United States and Britain watched the rise of Japan with growing alarm. Both had interests and territories which the new power of Japan put in danger. As a warning to Japan, they threatened to stop trading with her and cut down her oil supplies. While President Roosevelt was discussing these problems with the Japanese, they were secretly preparing to cripple the US Pacific Fleet.

The US Fleet on fire at Pearl Harbor. The Japanese surprised the Americans and the British with their skill in warfare and the quality of their weapons. At the beginning of the war they had ten fast, modern aircraft carriers and 2600 warplanes. This enabled them to win all the early battles.

President Roosevelt led the United States to victory. He made his country the most powerful nation in history.

## Pearl Harbor

In December 1941, United States and Japanese diplomats were talking about peace in the Pacific. At the same time, Japanese aircraft carriers were making a secret dash towards Pearl Harbor, Hawaii, the home of the US Pacific Fleet.

At dawn on 7 December, 350 planes took off from the carriers and headed for the unsuspecting US Fleet at anchor in the harbour. A radar operator warned that they were coming, but no-one took any notice. Within half an hour the Japanese had sunk 3 battleships, damaged 5 more and destroyed 188 aircraft parked on the ground.

The United States immediately declared war on Japan and the other Axis powers. Britain and her allies went to war with Japan. Now all the world was at war.

## The Eastern Conquest

The raid on Pearl Harbor put the US Fleet out of action. For a while, until the United States had made itself ready for war, the Japanese could do much as they liked in the Pacific. That is exactly what they had planned. They seized vast areas in a series of lightning conquests. Within six months they had taken the Philippines, Malaya, Singapore and Hong Kong, Burma, the Dutch East Indies and several British and US islands in the Pacific. They threatened to invade both India and Australia.

Japanese troops were trained to fight in jungles and to move rapidly on their own. The British and Americans found them hard to beat until they had learned to do the same. Japanese soldiers were also taught to die rather than surrender. The island of Tarawa had 4000 defenders. When the Americans recaptured it they took only 17 prisoners.

# Battle of the Atlantic

Britain needed vast quantities of raw materials, food, fuel and weapons to fight the war against Germany. These supplies came by ship across the Atlantic. The Germans reckoned that if they could stop the sea supplies from coming, Britain could not go on fighting. So the Atlantic became a major battleground.

U-boats (submarines) were Germany's chief weapons. In the early part of the war they sank hundreds of merchant vessels because Britain was short of warships to protect them. Slowly the British recovered. They used new equipment for detecting and sinking U-boats. The RAF used the Sunderland Flying Boat as its main submarine-hunter and sea-patrol aircraft of the war. It could stay in the air for 16 hours. Because it carried so many guns, the Germans called it the Flying Porcupine.

A U-boat stalks a British convoy. In September 1940, U-boats sank 27 ships in convoy SC7. Those ships were carrying:
- 200 tanks
- 670 guns
- 120 armoured cars
- 250 troop carriers
- 26,000 tonnes of ammunition
- 3000 rifles
- 2100 tonnes of tank supplies
- 10,000 tonnes of food
- 5000 tanks of petrol

Convoy PQ 17 sailed for Russia, laden with cargoes of vital war materials, on 27 June 1942. Of the 36 ships which set out, only 11 got through. The other 25 had been sunk in the icy Arctic waters north of Norway, by German aircraft and U-boats. No wonder the Arctic run was regarded as the most hazardous of all convoy duties. Altogether, British and US ships carried 4 million tonnes of war supplies to Russia, plus 5000 tanks and 7000 aircraft.

The Sunderland Flying Boat patrolled the oceans, hunting U-boats.

With American help, more ships and aircraft were available to hunt submarines. The U-boats were never completely beaten, but by the end of the war they could no longer threaten Britain with defeat.

## Sink the Bismarck

On 23 May 1941, the German battleship *Bismarck* was sighted. She was heading into the Atlantic towards Britain's vital supply lines. Immediately, every available British ship and aircraft was despatched to hunt her down.

The *Hood* and the *Prince of Wales* came upon the *Bismarck* the next day. The *Hood*, a twenty-year-old battlecruiser, was hit and blew up. The *Prince of Wales* was damaged and had to retire. But the *Bismarck* had been hit too and her captain decided to put into a French port for repairs.

Then torpedo aircraft from the carrier *Ark Royal* scored hits on the *Bismarck*. They damaged her propellers and jammed her rudder. Now she could not escape. Two British battleships pounded her into a blazing wreck. Torpedoes finally sent her to the bottom.

15

Germany's ally Italy began the desert war by attacking the small British army stationed in Egypt. The Italian dictator Mussolini planned to enlarge his North African empire by seizing Egypt and taking the Suez Canal.

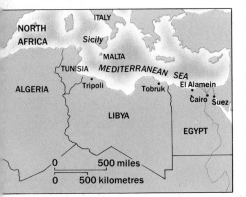

# The War in the Desert

The war in the desert moved back and forth for two years along the North African coast. In October 1942 the Germans, under General Rommel, and their Italian allies were deep inside Egypt. They were poised to take the Suez Canal, but the British and Commonwealth Eighth Army, led by General Montgomery, defeated them at El Alamein and drove them back into Libya.

Four days after Rommel began his retreat, a large force of US and British troops landed in Morocco and Algeria, under the command of the American General Eisenhower. It moved east to take Rommel and his Afrika Korps in the rear, but it was halted by fresh German troops hastily drafted in from Italy. This only delayed the inevitable Allied victory. Surrounded and outnumbered, a quarter of a million German and Italian troops surrendered on 12 May 1943.

## The Italian Campaign

From their bases in North Africa, the Allies now set out to invade Europe. Sicily was captured first. From there, on 3 September 1943, the Eighth Army crossed to the Italian mainland, and the Italians agreed to stop fighting. Many turned against the Germans and fought a dangerous war, behind the German lines, on the Allied side.

The Allies planned a swift advance up through Italy and on into the heart of Germany itself. Instead, they made slow and painful progress through rugged country, expertly defended by a determined enemy. It took them months of bitter and costly fighting to capture Cassino and open the road to the Italian capital Rome. The Americans liberated the city on 4 June 1944.

Allied bombers smashed the ancient abbey of Monte Cassino and turned it into a smoking ruin. But the German defenders fought on, from tunnels dug in the rock beneath the building. It took the Allies two more months of bitter fighting to drive them out.

By 1943, the Germans had 8876 of these 88mm flak guns defending their cities from Allied bombers. A million people, including women and schoolchildren, manned these defences.

**Avro Lancaster**
The four-engined Avro Lancaster carried up to ten tonnes of bombs at a height of 6500 metres. RAF Bomber Command used it as its main heavy night bomber from 1942 onwards.

# The Bomber Offensive

All-out bombing of Hitler's Germany began in 1943. The Americans bombed by day, the British by night. It was a round-the-clock attack.

At the beginning, the Allied aircraft often missed their targets, and many were shot down by German day- and night-fighters. The Germans quickly repaired damaged factories. Indeed, their industrial output went on rising to the end of the war. But by Autumn 1944 the Allies had overwhelmed the German defences and could find and hit targets anywhere in Germany with paralysing force.

Bombing did not win the war, as many leading airmen had hoped. The British did not give in when their cities were devastated by bombing. Neither did the Germans.

A German town lies in ruins. By late 1944, RAF Bomber Command was capable of terrifying destruction. In a single raid on Darmstadt, 218 Lancasters killed over 8000 people and utterly devastated half the town.

**Flying Fortress**
The US B17 Flying Fortress flew from bases in Britain to attack Hitler's Europe. Flying at 12,000 metres, it could hit the key targets with great accuracy.

**P51 Mustang**
The P51 Mustang was the best long-range fighter of the war. After it came into use as a bomber escort in late 1943, no part of Germany was safe from daylight bomber attack.

# The Final Advance

After his armies had failed to take Moscow, Hitler was determined to capture Stalingrad. He ignored advice from generals at the front who pleaded with him to destroy the Russian armies first. He sacked them and took command of the fighting himself – from Germany.

The Germans met ferocious resistance. The Russians made every building a fortress, every road a battlefield. The struggle went on, day and night, for five months.

Then, as the generals had warned, new Russian armies struck and cut off the Germans fighting in the city. All efforts to reach them failed. They were frozen and starving and had no ammunition. In February 1943, they surrendered.

When the German 6th Army in Stalingrad surrendered to the Russians, it was the worst defeat suffered by Hitler's Germany. The Germans lost half a million men in five months of fighting. It was a terrific blow to their war effort and to their pride.

The Russians hurried the attack on Berlin. They wanted to capture it before American or British troops could get there.

Two armies with over two million men made the final assault. By 25 April they had surrounded the city. On 2 May, the Russian red flag was hoisted over Berlin.

The Russian advance rolled on. As the year 1944 began, they drove away the Germans, who had cut off Leningrad from the rest of Russia, and freed the city. The siege of Leningrad had lasted 900 days and towards the end its people were dying of cold and hunger at the rate of 20,000 a week. At last, food, fuel and clothing could be rushed to its frozen and starving defenders.

By the summer of 1944, scattered groups of Germans were trying to hold back the Russian advance on a front of over 2000 kms. They had neither the men nor the weapons to do so. The Russians now began to enter countries which the Germans had conquered: Poland, Hungary, Romania, Bulgaria and last of all Czechoslovakia. In all these countries the Russians set up governments they knew would be friendly towards themselves. Thus, even before the war was over, Europe was being divided between East and West.

# Operation Overlord

**Eisenhower commanded the Allied invasion of Europe.**

The Allies assembled vast forces for Operation Overlord, the invasion of Europe. Altogether three million men were involved plus 10,000 aircraft, 1200 warships and over 5000 transports and landing craft. General Eisenhower was Supreme Commander and General Montgomery commanded the initial landing. Early June 1944 was chosen for D-Day. Airborne troops were to go in first and hold off the Germans, while one United States and one British and Canadian army stormed ashore and established beachheads.

The Allies had to land enormous quantities of stores of all kinds on the Normandy beaches to support the invasion force. Landing craft which could sail in very shallow water came right up to the beaches to deliver loads of food, ammunition, tanks, lorries and self-propelled guns.

The night of 5 June 1944 was stormy, but the weather men forecast that the seas would be calm by morning. General Eisenhower trusted them, and gave the order for Overlord to begin. Early on 6 June warships and bombers battered the massive defences of Hitler's Atlantic Wall between the River Seine and Cherbourg. At 6.30 am the first assault troops and tanks landed on the beaches.

The attack caught the Germans unprepared. They thought the weather was too bad for a landing. Within 48 hours the Allies had fought their way through the Atlantic Wall and begun the build-up for the long advance into Germany.

# The Collapse of Japan

The attack on Pearl Harbor put most of the US Pacific Fleet out of action. But the aircraft carriers were at sea at the time and were not touched. This was an enormous stroke of luck for the Americans, since carriers were the ships that won the war in the Pacific.

At the first major battle between the Japanese and US Navies, in the Coral Sea, the two fleets never met. Both lost an aircraft carrier, sunk by carrier aircraft from the other side. In June, US carrier aircraft off Midway Island sank all four Japanese carriers sent to attack them. It was the beginning of the end for the Japanese in the Pacific.

The Americans killed over 100,000 Japanese when they captured Okinawa. They lost 12,500 dead of their own men. The Japanese sent pilots out on suicide missions, to sink US ships by flying their aircraft into them. They were called Kamikazes. Over 4000 of them were used, and died, at Okinawa.

The Americans now began to attack the islands in the Pacific on the way to Japan itself. There were terrible losses on both sides, as the Japanese fought to the death or launched themselves in suicide attacks.

In South East Asia, the British threw back a Japanese invasion of India. In New Guinea, Australian and American troops, fighting in thick jungle where previously the Japanese soldier had been unbeatable, drove off a Japanese force and ended the threat to Australia.

## The Atomic Bomb

The Americans began to move in on Japan. One by one, Japanese islands out in the Pacific were captured. Each island was defended by Japanese soldiers who went on killing until they were killed themselves. The US leaders knew that the biggest and most costly battle would be the attack on Japan itself. They estimated that over a million American soldiers alone would die in the fighting.

On 16 July 1945 the US tested the first atomic bomb. They saw its devastating power and decided to use it against Japan to terrify the Japanese into asking for peace. If this was successful, it would not be necessary to invade Japan and millions of lives would be saved.

Dropping the bomb was easy. American bombers could now attack Japan much as they pleased. On 6 August they took the first bomb, called Little Boy, to Hiroshima. In an instant, a vast area of the city vanished. But the Japanese did not give in. On 9 August a second bomb, called Fat Man, wiped out most of Nagasaki.

Japan surrendered on 14 August. The next day, Japanese troops everywhere heard their Emperor tell them on the radio to cease fighting. The Second World War was over.

On 6 August 1945, the first atom bomb dropped on Japan. It destroyed Hiroshima and killed 70,000 people. Three days later, the second bomb fell, on Nagasaki, killing 80,000 people. We shall never know how many more died of burns, wounds or radiation sickness.

# After the War

Two olive branches meaning 'peace' hold the world between them on the United Nations flag.

Nearly all the countries in the world belong to the General Assembly of the United Nations. They meet once a year in New York.

The war made many changes to the world. The empires which had given Britain and France great influence soon passed away. Germany and Japan, both ruined by the war, were occupied by armies of the victorious nations. Germany was divided, and has since become two countries, separated by a frontier-long barrier.

Western Europe no longer led the world. Its place was taken by Russia and the United States, which came out of the war as the superpowers of the future.

The statesmen of the victorious powers met in 1945 to plan a better future for all people. They resolved to set up an organisation which would keep order in the world and prevent a major war from breaking out again. It was called the United Nations Organisation.

The Berlin Wall: over three million skilled workers and others left East Germany for the West up to 1961. The East Germans could not afford to lose such people and they built a wall to stop them. It runs for 42 kms through Berlin. A high fence stretches 1400kms across the whole of Germany.

# Important Events and People of World War II

**1933**
Jan   Hitler and the Nazi
party come to power.

**1933-38**
Hitler secretly builds up
German armed forces.

**1938**
March   Hitler takes over
Austria.
Sept   Hitler seizes part of
Czechoslovakia.
Oct   Chamberlain returns
from meeting with Hitler
in Munich and claims to
bring 'peace for our
time'.
Dec   Nazis begin savage
persecution of the Jews.

**Neville Chamberlain
was British Prime Minister
when war began. When his
policies failed, he was
succeeded by Winston
Churchill.**

**1939**
March   Germans take the
rest of Czechoslovakia.
May 22   Germany and Italy
become allies.
Aug 23   Germany and Russia
make secret pact to share
Poland between them.
Sept 1   Germany invades
Poland.
        3   Britain and France
declare war on Germany;
Australia, New Zealand
and Canada follow.
        17   Russians invade
Poland.
Oct 6   Poles stop fighting.

**1940**
April 9   Germans invade
Denmark and Norway.
May 10   Germans invade
Holland and Belgium.
Chamberlain resigns and
Churchill becomes Prime
Minister of Britain.
        26   Evacuation of Allied
troops from Dunkirk
begins.
June 3   Dunkirk evacuation
ends.
        10   Italy declares war on
France and Britain.
Norway surrenders to the
Germans.
        14   German army enters
Paris.

**General Heinz Guderian
invented blitzkrieg warfare.
He led Panzer attacks in
France and Russia.**

        17   Pétain, the new
premier of France,
surrenders to the
Germans.
        18   De Gaulle forms
Free French Government
in London.
July 10   Battle of Britain
begins.
        16   Hitler plans invasion
of Britain for mid-
August.
Aug 12   Eagle Day: massive
Luftwaffe attack on
Britain.
        25   RAF bomb Berlin.
Sept 7   London bombed at
night. Beginning of the
Blitz.

15   Battle of Britain Sunday. RAF smash German attacks on London.
17   Hitler calls off the invasion of Britain.
Dec 9   British offensive in Desert War.

**1941**
Mar 24   Rommel counter-attacks in Desert War.
April 6   Germans invade Greece and Yugoslavia.
May 24   *Bismarck* sinks HMS *Hood*.
27   Royal Navy sinks *Bismarck*.

**Joseph Stalin was absolute ruler of Russia. Single-minded in his determination to defeat Germany, he made Russia a superpower.**

halted 30 kms from Moscow.
Dec 5   Surprise Russian counter-attack at Moscow. Germans suffer in freezing weather.
7   Japan raids US naval base at Pearl Harbor. US, Britain and allies now at war with Germany, Italy and Japan.
25   Hong Kong falls to Japan.

**1942**
Jan 5   Major Russian offensive begins. Germans retreat.
Feb 15   Singapore surrenders to Japanese.
19   Heavy raids on Darwin by Japanese aircraft.

May 2   Japanese complete conquest of Burma.
4   Coral Sea battle between US and Japan
17   Germans halt Russian advance.
30   First RAF 1000 bomber raid on Germany (Cologne).
June 4   Battle of Midway. US Navy cripples Japanese fleet.
July 1   Rommel reaches El Alamein.

**Admiral Karl Doenitz planned and ran the U-boat campaign. He briefly succeeded Hitler as leader of Germany.**

June 22   Germans invade Russia.
June–Nov   Germans advance into Russia.
Nov 26   German Panzers

**Field Marshal Erwin Rommel commanded German Afrika Korps in Desert War in N Africa. Organised defence of Europe against Allied invasion in 1944.**

Aug 7   US begins to move in on Japan. Marines land on Guadalcanal Island.
19   First German attack on Stalingrad.
Oct 23–Nov 4   Montgomery attacks at El Alamein.

Germans retreat to
Libya.
Nov 8   Combined US/British
invasion of N Africa.

### 1943
Jan 23   Eighth Army enters
Tripoli.
31   Germans surrender
in Stalingrad.
Feb–Nov   Russians advance
along whole front
towards Germany.
May 12   Germans surrender
to Allies in N Africa.
July 10   Allies invade Sicily.
12   German Panzers
defeated at Kursk.
Sep 3   Allies invade Italian
mainland.
8   Italian government
surrenders. German
army takes control in
Italy.

**General George Patton
was the foremost American
tank general of the war. He
led the American advance
across France in 1944.**

### 1944
Jan 4   Russians advance into
Poland.
May 18   Allies capture
Cassino.
June 4   Allies liberate Rome.
6   D-Day: Allies land in
Normandy.
July 20   Plot to kill Hitler
fails.
31   Allies begin major
advance in N France.
Aug 25   De Gaulle enters
Paris.

**General Charles de Gaulle
escaped from France in
1940 to lead French
resistance against Germany.**

Sep 3   Brussels liberated.
11   US Army enters
Germany.
17   Airborne attack on
Arnhem bridge fails.
Dec 16   Germans counter-
attack in the Ardennes.

### 1945
Jan 17   Russians capture
Warsaw.
28   End of German
attack in the Ardennes.
Mar 7   US troops cross the
Rhine.
April 1   Americans attack
Okinawa.
12   President Roosevelt
dies; Truman succeeds
him.
26   Russian and
American troops meet in
Germany.
28   Italians shoot
Mussolini.
29   Germans surrender
in Italy.
30   Hitler kills himself.
May 7   VE Day. Germans
surrender.
Aug 6   Atom bomb dropped
on Hiroshima.
9   Second bomb
dropped on Nagasaki.
14   Japan surrenders.
15   VJ Day. Britain and
America celebrate end of
war.

# Index